ARTS AND CRAFTS FURNITURE AND METALWORK

A QUANTUM BOOK

Published by Grange Books
an imprint of Grange Books Plc
The Grange
Kingsnorth Industrial Estate
Hoo, nr. Rochester
Kent ME3 9ND

1-84013-263-9

This book is produced by
Quantum Books Ltd
6 Blundell Street
London N7 9BH

Project Manager: Rebecca Kingsley
Project Editor: Judith Millidge
Designer: Wayne Humphries
Editor: Clare Haworth-Maden

The material in this publication previously appeared in
The Arts and Crafts Movement, Encyclopedia of Furniture

QUMACFM
Set in Times
Reproduced in Singapore by Eray Scan (Pte) Ltd
Printed in Singapore by Star Standard Industries (Pte) Ltd

CONTENTS

INTRODUCTION

On 1 May 1851 Britain celebrated its industrial might with the opening of the 'Great Exhibition of all Nations'. The exhibition took place in Joseph Paxton's Crystal Palace, erected in London's Hyde Park. The glass and iron construction, some 1,800ft (549m) long, 140ft (43m) high and with a volume of 33 million cubic ft (934,000 cubic m), was erected in less than eight months.

Opposite: Joseph Paxton's innovative, pre-fabricated, iron-and-glass Crystal Palace, which housed the Great Exhibition of 1851.

Below: New machinery on show at the 1851 Great Exhibition.

Sir Matthew Digby, secretary to the exhibition's executive committee, saw this vast undertaking as a reflection of the national character. The size of the venture represented national courage, and the nation's strength could be seen in the speed with which it was built. National wealth was displayed in the resources used in the building, and the country's intellect was symbolised by its architectural complexity. Moreover, the beauty of the Crystal Palace, according to Digby, demonstrated that 'the British are by no means indifferent to the beautiful in fine arts'. The building housed the work of 15,000 exhibitors, which was displayed in four categories: raw materials, machinery, manufactures, and sculpture and the fine arts. Queen Victoria summed up the exhibition's purpose in her reply to her husband's opening address. She hoped that it would 'conduce to . . . the common interests of the human race by encouraging the arts of peace and industry', and that it would promote 'friendly and honourable rivalry . . . for the good and happiness of mankind'.

THE MISERY OF INDUSTRIALISATION

Many of Victoria's subjects did not share her appreciation for the fruits of industry and free international trade and saw the onslaught of industrialisation as detrimental to the nation. Since the beginning of the nineteenth century, many commentators had realised that industry had the capacity to generate wealth and misery in equal quantities. William Cobbett, writing as early as 1807, observed that the industrialised city of Coventry maintained a population of 20,000, almost one half of which were paupers. Industry had generated wealth but concentrated that wealth in the hands of a few people, serving to create 'two nations'.

The sense of loyalty and social responsibility that was understood to have existed between the various levels of society in the previous centuries was now absent. The creed of *laissez-faire* utilitarianism relieved the wealthy from any responsibility towards the poor. Some economists saw the conditions that

Above: Pencil sketch of Edward Burne-Jones by Simeon Solomon, 1850.

Right: Luke Fildes, Applicants for Admission to a Casual Labour Ward, *oil on canvas, 1874.*

Cobbett, Engels and others described as an unfortunate but necessary evil. Social life in England was, in the eyes of many critics, gradually being undermined to generate a nation of masters and wage-slaves.

VOICES OF DISSENT

The climate of dissent in the late eighteenth and nineteenth centuries took on a variety of forms. At one end of the spectrum was the romantic, celibate 'brotherhood' dedicated to art and chivalry, as conceived by William Morris (1834–96) and Edward Burne-Jones (1833–98) while at Oxford. This fraternity devoted itself to things of the spirit and determined to mask the horrors of industrialism beneath a veneer of art. At the other end of the spectrum, Karl Marx and Friedrich Engels saw within industrial society's class struggle inevitable revolution and the seeds of its own destruction. At various points between these extremes a host of other critics argued for democratic freedom and the emancipation of the industrial working classes or saw national salvation in the revival of the feudal ideals of a lost past. In many instances there was very little love lost between the factions. These dissenters, whether revolutionary or romantic, were, however, bound by the deep suspicion that was to be shared by artists and artisans of the Arts and Crafts Movement, the suspicion that society under industrialism was getting worse rather than better.

ROMANTIC ESCAPISM

During the first half of the nineteenth century protests against the horror of the Industrial Revolution were common. The tone of these

Right: William Morris pictured aged 23, when he was at Oxford.

protests was often ineffectual, serving to create a means of escape from the unpleasantness of Victorian life rather than a remedy for its social ills. Aspects of some of the earlier paintings of Dante Gabriel Rossetti (1828–82) and his contemporaries and the poetry of William Morris serve as examples in which refined artistic sensibilities were used to eclipse the realities of the world. In essence, imagination afforded a romantic shelter from real life.

LITERARY CATALYSTS

Protests against industrialism attained a stronger and intellectually more coherent character in the writings of two of the most important catalysts of the Arts and Crafts Movement, Thomas Carlyle (1795–1881) and John Ruskin (1819–1900). Both Carlyle and Ruskin were read avidly by the young Morris while at Oxford, and Ruskin in particular was to exert

Above: The Girlhood of Mary Virgin, *by Dante Gabriel Rossetti, 1848.*

Right: Christ in the House of His Parents, *by John Everett Millais, 1850.*

Below: Thomas Carlyle, *by A C Armytage.*

a strong influence on the Pre-Raphaelites, their counterparts in the United States and on the development of the Arts and Crafts Movement on both sides of the Atlantic. Neither Carlyle nor Ruskin shared the socialist convictions of many of those active within the Arts and Crafts Movement. Both writers were conservative and Carlyle, at times, was deeply reactionary. The movement, however, gleaned from them a marked distaste for modern industrial capitalism that went beyond the sentimental and gradually began to take on a practical, philosophical form.

THOMAS CARLYLE

Carlyle's invective against the horrors of the modern age was directed at the twin evils of mechanised industrial society and the radical movements that had risen to oppose it. Utilitarianism, he said, demanded that if machinery proved a more efficient instrument of profit it should be used regardless of the consequences to less efficient human labour. Absent in both utilitarianism and its Chartist antidote was the old feudal notion of social responsibility and a sense of community explained by Carlyle in *Chartism*. The solution could be found in the restoration of a socially responsible hierarchy led by the 'strong of heart' and 'noble of soul'. In essence, the restoration of these conditions could be found in a return to the chivalric ideals of medieval England. The restoration of these conditions would ensure that the serf would work under the paternalistic protection of the lord; labour would be dignified and bonds of mutual co-operation would replace the chains of industry wherein wage-slaves were bound to inanimate machines in their desperate need for cash.

Above: John Ruskin, an early photograph.

Right: A drawing of Rouen Cathedral, by John Ruskin, c. 1850. Ruskin, whose writings on art and architecture influenced William Morris so much, was a fine amateur artist.

JOHN RUSKIN

John Ruskin placed a similar emphasis on the value of work, in particular on the value of creative work. The 'machine age', he argued, had created a division of labour in which it was impossible for men and women to find fulfilment in work. He objected to the refinement of contemporary Victorian design because it was dependent upon machinery, and machinery necessarily destroyed the creativity of human labour. Ruskin was less sentimental than many of his contemporaries about the charms of a medieval past. He nonetheless maintained that work in the Middle Ages, although hard and often unpleasant, was

undertaken voluntarily by men and women and retained its dignity.

The dignity found in simple and unsophisticated craftsmanship explains Ruskin's unbridled admiration for medieval building. He recognised the 'fantastic ignorance' of the sculptors who had decorated medieval churches and conceded the sophistication of his age in comparison to that of the past. He nonetheless saw the conditions under which medieval craftsmen worked as infinitely more wholesome than the mechanised drudgery of industrialism and maintained that it was to the spirit of this medieval model that nineteenth-century society must turn for salvation. Production, he insisted, would be for use rather than profit and machine-like precision would be exchanged for an imperfect human finish.

A W N PUGIN

One of the first architects and designers in Britain to give practical form to an antipathy for the modern industrial environment was A W N Pugin (1812–52). Pugin employed an architectural style reminiscent of that of the Middle Ages. He distinguished himself from many late eighteenth- and early nineteenth-century Gothic revivalists by equating the appearance of medieval building with the spiritual refinement of the Middle Ages. The Gothic style had long been employed, either for its picturesque characteristics or as a nationalistic antidote to the international classical style. Pugin, however, maintained that Gothic was less a style than an architectural representation of Christian sentiment and was starkly contrasted to the crass and spiritually vacuous utilitarian building of his own age.

Although Ruskin and Morris dissociated themselves from Pugin (respectively for his Catholicism and his antipathy to working-class movements), the notion that art and architecture carry the capacity to redeem and improve society was an important departure in Gothic Revivalist architecture and one that was to recur in many manifestations of the Arts and Crafts Movement, both in Europe and the United States.

AMERICAN GOTHIC

Mid-nineteenth-century America began to share the European taste for Gothic architecture. In most cases American builders used the Gothic purely for its picturesque and visual appearance. James Renwick Jr, for example, designer of Grace Church on New York's

Above: A W N Pugin's work in the Gothic Revival style often rivalled the original models in authenticity.

Left: Maiolica plate designed by A W N Pugin, c. 1850.

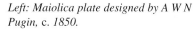

Above: 'The Hôtel de Ville, Paris,' from A W N Pugin's Contrasts, *published in 1836.*

Right: A detail of Lyndhurst, the mansion built in Tarrytown, New York, by Alexander Jackson Davis.

Lower Broadway and the Smithsonian Institution in Washington, DC, used the Gothic with little regard for the historical associations that the style retained in Britain. Some architects, however, began to adapt and lend their own meaning to the style. The Gothic was seen by some as less pretentious than the sophisticated Greek Revival style that had dominated American building in the early nineteenth century.

Andrew Jackson Downing (1815–51), a landscape gardener and writer, saw within the Gothic style an element of honesty and practicality. The style was, he maintained, far better suited to the homespun aspirations of American citizens and could also serve to refine uneducated American tastes, cheapened by the mass-produced *objets d'art* that had flooded markets in the wake of the Industrial Revolution in the United States. Downing advocated, in some instances, the use of a more elaborate Gothic style in the design of homes for the wealthy. In general, however, he believed that good domestic American architecture could take its lead from the example set by more modest Tudor, Gothic or Tuscan building, simple but soundly built architecture appropriate to the independent lifestyle of most rural Americans.

JAMES JACKSON JARVES
The notion of a specifically American sense of design and architecture was developed in the writings of the art collector and critic James Jackson Jarves (1818–88). Jarves, a keen collector of late-medieval Italian paintings, disliked the way in which European styles were being inappropriately used for American building to create 'chaotic, incomplete, and arbitrary' architecture. Eschewing both 'bastard Grecian' and 'impoverished Gothic',

Jarves advocated an independent path that was to be followed by architects and designers associated with the Arts and Crafts Movement in both Europe and the United States. Building, Jarves insisted, must be in harmony with its surroundings. He maintained that architecture grew out of the wants and ideas of a nation and could not be imported at will from a well of European styles and influence, be they Greek, Roman or Gothic.

ARCHITECTURAL PROPONENTS
The development of a sense of artistic independence and the return to the commonsense values of the pioneer primarily occurred in writing rather than in shingle, bricks and mortar. There are some exceptions, however, including the architects Alexander Jackson Davis and Richard Upjohn. Davis, a friend of

Left: Rotch House, New Bedford, Massachusetts, by Alexander Jackson Davis, 1850.

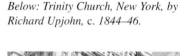

Below: Trinity Church, New York, by Richard Upjohn, c. 1844–46.

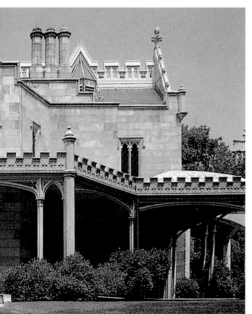

Downing, abhorred the symmetry of Greek classicism, preferring the more modest Gothic style. Two contrasting examples of his work are the large mansion Lyndhurst, built in Tarrytown, New York, and the less ambitious Rotch House, a comparatively small cottage in New Bedford, Massachusetts. Upjohn – architect of Trinity Church on New York's Broadway – contributed to a more sophisticated understanding of Gothic architecture not dissimilar to that of Pugin, seeing the Gothic style as an idiom uniquely able to communicate Christian feeling. Architecture was seen as a medium of faith.

THE DEVELOPMENT OF THE ARTS AND CRAFTS MOVEMENT

The Arts and Crafts Movement in Britain and the United States was thus built on separate but by no means independent cultural traditions. In Britain, the idea of a

Above: According to Arts and Crafts reformers, many nineteenth-century factories utilised a 'division of labour' to increase the speed of production.

Above right: A Gothic sideboard, in ebonised wood with painted and leather panels, designed by Philip Webb, c. 1862.

Below right: Josef Hoffmann, a founder of the Wiener Werkstätte, designed this elegant coffee pot.

pre-industrial, medieval past articulated through the writings of Ruskin, Carlyle and Pugin provided the British Arts and Crafts Movement with a strong sense of the artistic, moral and social refinements of a technologically less sophisticated age. This British ideal of a feudal past has an American counterpart in the image of the pioneer. The traditions according to which the American Arts and Crafts Movement developed were those of a respect for work, independence and self-sufficiency and the desire to fashion a national culture remote from the fanciful notions and historical traditions of the Old World – Europe.

These two separate but linked traditions, which shared a distaste for sophistication, a strong sense of independence and a belief in the sanctity of work – ideals embodied in the furniture and metalwork explored in this book – were respectively to determine the shape of the Arts and Crafts Movement in Britain and the United States throughout the remainder of the nineteenth century and also into the twentieth century.

ARTS AND CRAFTS
FURNISHINGS

Previous page: The William Morris Room in the Victoria & Albert Museum, London. The windows are by Burne-Jones; the screen by Jane and William Morris; the piano's gesso work by Kate Faulkner; and the walls by Philip Webb.

Opposite: The drawing room at Standen; the chair with cushions in the foreground is by Morris & Co, as are the hand-knotted carpet and wallpaper.

Below: Title page from Clarence Cook's The House Beautiful, *1878, which introduced tasteful art and design to the American bourgeoisie.*

'**Have nothing in your homes that you do not know to be useful or believe to be beautiful**', advised William Morris. Indeed, the Arts and Crafts Movement was first and foremost an effort to reform the domestic environment, and design reformers obeyed Morris by eliminating the superfluous and unsightly from their surroundings. They were single-minded in their purpose, hoping to improve living conditions and thereby also to strengthen the character of the individual.

But they differed in their approach, as there was no clear-cut path to follow in achieving their goal. Consequently, Arts and Crafts interiors vary greatly, from minute detail to overall character. They are similar in that all unite the useful with the beautiful, yet they are different, as each is a unique expression of a particular set of influences, including designer, client, time, period, location, as well as cultural milieu.

ARTS AND CRAFTS INTERIOR STYLE
An Arts and Crafts interior can best be defined by establishing what it is not. It is never pretentious or intimidating in its scale, arrangements or textures. It shuns overly realistic patterns, shoddy craftsmanship and imitation materials. It is not slavishly imitative in its use of historical models, nor is it overburdened with archaeological motifs or classical ornamentation. It is seldom stylistically pure and, above all, it rejects the worldly trappings of its other Victorian contemporaries.

In these and other ways, the Arts and Crafts interior contrasts markedly with other Victorian examples. It is a product of the nineteenth century, yet it rejects many Victorian conventions governing aesthetics, construction and materials. For these reasons, the Arts and Crafts interior is viewed as a precursor to the Modern Movement. It illustrates the first important stage in the evolution from the nineteenth-century aesthetic of conspicuous consumption to the twentieth-century argument that less is more.

AN INFLUENTIAL INTERIOR: RED HOUSE
The prerequisite characteristics of the Arts and Crafts interior were introduced by Philip Webb in Red House, Bexley Heath, in Kent, designed in 1859 for William Morris and his bride, Jane Burden. In designing this innovative structure, Webb established several fundamental principles which influenced, to one degree or another, every subsequent Arts and Crafts interior designed over the next 70 years.

The first principle demonstrated by Red House is that in form, ornament and material each interior must be a logical outgrowth of structure and plan. The second principle is that each interior must have a distinctive character befitting its particular function, but it must, at the same time, provide a variation upon a greater theme which links room to room. The third principle is that each interior must reveal its structural components honestly. The fourth principle is that each interior must use appropriate materials with integrity, from broadest surface to smallest detail.

Besides establishing these important principles, Red House presents a striking lesson

Top: Red House, Bexley Heath, Kent.

Above: The entry/stair hall, Red House.

pre-industrial look often did not incorporate much actual handwork, particularly in later years. But the ideal and symbolism were all important. From hand-sawn planks and hand-blocked wallpapers to metals pockmarked by the planishing hammer or corners enlivened by the draw knife, the surfaces of the Arts and Crafts interior highlight the skilled touch of

in the application of historical models for contemporary use. The house reflects the shared passion of both architect and client for the Middle Ages, but it does so with modified, vernacular forms and simplified Gothic ornamentation. Both form and ornament acknowledge a historical source but update its essential characteristics for use in a mid-nineteenth-century dwelling.

THE ARTS AND CRAFTS CHARACTER
Every interior of the design-reform movement has a distinctive character, determined by such factors as cultural influences and local context. They can therefore appear collectively more different than one another than similar. But they nevertheless share several commonalities regarding the use of materials, the selection of patterns and finishes and the inclusion of certain planning features.

One similarity is the appearance of hand-craftsmanship, although this rustic, the artisan or craftsman. These handcrafted finishes replace the lifeless, machine-produced veneers of the Victorian era. They are testimonies to the process of 'man'-ufacture and, as such, are signatures of the individual worker. They are evidence of the maker's personality which, in turn, makes an Arts and Crafts interior even more personable.

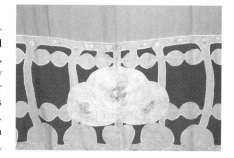

Left: 'Trellis' wallpaper, designed by Morris and Webb, first produced in 1862.

Centre left: The attic bedroom of William Morris' Kelmscott Manor, with green-stained furniture by Madox Brown, c. 1861.

Below: Hanging (detail) worked in silk on linen by Ann Macbeth, Glasgow, Scotland, c. 1900.

NATURAL MATERIALS

In most Arts and Crafts interiors, such handcrafted finishes appear in tandem with informal materials and textures. Rough-cut stone, rough-hewn beams, seeded glass, grainy woods and plain-woven wools, linens or cottons replace the polished, fragile textures associated with formal, high-style interiors. These humble, inviting materials are used in a fashion that accentuates their imperfections. They are durable and have been chosen to age gracefully. They welcome, and are enhanced by, daily interaction with the user.

While Arts and Crafts interiors glorify handcrafted finishes and informal textures, they also demonstrate a traditional approach to the construction of architectural elements and furnishings. Timbered ceilings evoke the framing techniques of the early housewright. Cut-stone floors, walls and fireplaces demonstrate the painstaking methods of the mason. Spindled backs recall the skills of the

Right: 'Evenlode' printed cotton, indigo discharged, designed by Morris and registered in 1883, the first of the Morris designs to be named after a tributary of the Thames.

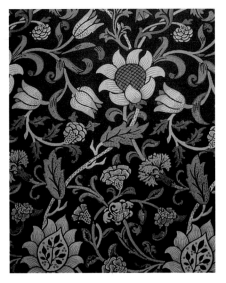

Below: An interior view of Hill House, Dunbartonshire, Scotland, designed by Charles Rennie Mackintosh, 1904.

Windsor-chair-maker, and panelling, storage pieces and seat furniture made of solid woods with exposed joints reflect the techniques of the early joiner and turner. Even the approach to ornamentation tends to be traditional: run-mouldings, incised lines, chip-carving or painting add interest to surfaces when structural polychromatic or integrated patterns are not already sufficient. In Arts and Crafts interiors, the forms of elements and furnishings might be progressive in their suave simplicity, but the manner in which they are wrought, assembled and embellished is nevertheless often retrospective.

DECORATIVE MOTIFS

Their provincial sympathies are exemplified by the decorative motifs found on surfaces, textiles, furnishings and objects: many are of humble origin, associated for generations with the folk tradition. The decorative vocabulary consists of simple, geometrical shapes and conventionalised natural motifs, used individually or as repetitive patterns or borders. Popular devices include the tulip, rose, leaf and bird. But chief among these is the heart, which appears on forms as diverse as leaded glass by Will Bradley, cupboards by Charles Rennie Mackintosh, chair backs by C F A Voysey and firedogs by Ernest Gimson.

Justifications for the popularity of these folk motifs are at least threefold. Firstly, they are compatible stylistically with the provincial nature of many Arts and Crafts designs. Secondly, they are as simple and direct in form as are the shapes and surfaces that they embellish. And thirdly, they evoke the positive, homely virtues that design reformers hoped to restore to daily life. But they are by no means used in a simplistic fashion: rather, they are manipulated in a sophisticated manner which belies their humble origins. In the hands of an accomplished designer, they assume an air of calculated *naïveté*.

Equally sophisticated are the patterns that are derived from natural sources and are often regional in their character. Morris' distinctive chintzes, wallpapers and carpets immortalise the wild flowers and vegetation growing along streams and in country gardens in south-eastern England. Mackintosh's sinuous wall stencils and embroideries provide variations upon the traditional Glasgow rose, which flourishes in Scotland's grey, damp climate. Frank Lloyd Wright's stained-glass windows, lighting fixtures and carpets capture with angular precision the essence of weeds, seed pods and trees growing wild on the prairies of the American Midwest. And Candace Wheeler's appliqués

and tapestries transform in subtle tone-on-tone the thistles, pine cones, ivy and shells of the north-eastern United States. All of these have a freshness and originality that results from a close observation of nature. But, by virtue of colour, composition, scale and modelling, they are transformed from the commonplace into the extraordinary.

CREATING WARMTH AND LIGHT

In dimension, Arts and Crafts interiors range from grand to modest, yet all are inviting and approachable. Such qualities are the combined result of finishes and furnishings, but they are due as well to conventions regarding fenestration and planning. Like the interiors of the late Middle Ages, or those of the Elizabethan age, Arts and Crafts interiors express a desire

Above: A fireplace in an upstairs drawing room, Red House, Bexley Heath, by Philip Webb, 1859–60. In shape, this fireplace resembles those found in medieval castles.

Left: The drawing room at Kelmscott Manor. The armchairs are covered with 'Peacock and Dragon', a woven woollen fabric designed by Morris.

Above: A design for a living room by M H Baillie-Scott, 1911.

Right: An artist's impression of a dining room, published in The Craftsman *by Stickley's United Crafts, 1904.*

for light and warmth. In pursuit of such attributes, architects identified as priorities the size, shape and placement of windows and the location of the fireplace, the focal point within most spaces.

THE INGLENOOK

The fireplace was the hub of domestic activity, and its stature as such was frequently augmented by structural furnishings or fire-side windows. Known as an inglenook, this enclosed fireplace bay became an intimate room-within-a-room. Its cosiness was often accentuated by a lowered ceiling or raised floor level. The importance of the inglenook as an Arts and Crafts planning feature was recognised by the German architect and critic Hermann Muthesius, who traced its origins to Anglo-Saxon homes in his influential book of 1904–5, *The English House.*

The treatment of the inglenook varies, but it can be found in 'reformed' interiors throughout Europe and America. It appears in cottages and country estates designed by C F A Voysey; in the Prairie-style homes and 'Craftsman' bungalows of Frank Lloyd Wright or Gustav Stickley; in the Aesthetic or Colonial Revival interiors of the north-eastern United States; and in the Glasgow-style rooms by Mackintosh and his American emulator Will Bradley. The inglenook is a ubiquitous feature in entrance halls, stair halls, drawing rooms and dining rooms. It serves both a practical and a decorative purpose, but, above all, it is significant for its symbolic connotation: it is the heart of the Arts and Crafts interior and is often located at the centre of the plan. Its symbolic importance may explain the prevalence of the heart-shaped motif on the hoods, implements and furniture used in its proximity.

CEILINGS AND FRIEZES

The intimate atmosphere of the Arts and Crafts interior is often determined by the ceiling, which is purposefully lowered or detailed to accentuate the horizontality of the room. A lowered ceiling is often complemented by an ornamental frieze, a decorative horizontal strip defining the upper third of the wall. The frieze is frequently painted with a narrative mural or a large-scale repetitive border, but it might just as often be covered with stencilling or wallpaper to distinguish it from the wall surface below. In the nursery, it might include a motto or inscription, carefully selected to mould the character of the room's youthful occupant. The

frieze in such cases becomes a permanent work of art, integrated into the very structure of the building's interior.

The frieze may, on the other hand, be plain, to contrast with built-in furniture, fabric, wallpaper or panelling below. A plain frieze is often trimmed with a picture moulding, plate rail or shallow ledge used to support small watercolours or prints, ceramics or carefully selected *bric-à-brac*. Defined by the frieze, these decorative elements appear as an extension of the interior architecture rather than as distracting foreground clutter. The plain frieze can have a practical purpose as well: Voysey advocated the use of a light-coloured frieze

to reflect natural daylight. Others, such as Wright, extended a frieze of uniform width from room to room to establish visual continuity throughout a structure.

A UNIFIED ENSEMBLE

Such continuity is perhaps the most striking and, indeed, the most universal aspect among interiors of the design-reform movement. Finishes, textures, patterns and other elements might vary according to the demands of a client, but the architect always strove to unite the interior from large scale to small. Each was viewed as an ensemble, to be co-ordinated from background to furnishings to accessories. A unified result depended on the sensitive eye of the designer, who had to pay attention to every detail of the interior while orchestrating the whole.

Despite such commonalities, Arts and Crafts interiors differ greatly in overall appearance. They range from subtle to brilliant, from Spartan to crowded and overstuffed, and from eclectic to stylistically pure. They express a universal quest for logic, unity,

Above: The drawing room, Standen, Sussex, by Philip Webb, 1892–94.

Below: The dining room of the Palais Stoclet, designed by Josef Hoffmann and incorporating marble veneers and mosaics by Gustav Klimt.

Above: The drawing room, Wightwick Manor, Staffordshire, by Edward Ould, 1887. The heaviness of the interior architectural features is counteracted by the products from Morris & Co, eighteenth-century antiques and oriental porcelains.

honesty and integrity in design, yet each presents a personal interpretation of usefulness and beauty.

THE USE OF COLOUR

Colour, as one component of beauty, is treated variously by Arts and Crafts architects and designers. Voysey, M H Baillie Scott, Carl Larsson and Bradley include large blocks of vivid colour to define interior planes boldly. Others, such as Mackintosh or Josef Hoffmann, utilise an achromatic palette of whites, greys and blacks enlivened with strategic touches of brilliant colour. Another group offers a conservative approach: Philip Webb, Edward Ould, Stanford White and Henry Hobson Richardson incorporate chintzes, wallpapers or oriental rugs as subtle, multi-coloured accents. The majority, however, eliminate bright colour altogether, choosing instead to emphasise the dull tones of structural materials, such as wood, stone, brick, plaster, metal or leather.

TEXTILES

Like colour, textiles are partially responsible for the usefulness and beauty of an Arts and

Crafts interior. In some interiors, every form is padded and every surface draped, while in later interiors and those designed by architects fabric and cushioning are kept to a minimum. The relative presence or absence of those elements affects profoundly the overall character of the room.

In some Arts and Crafts interiors, textiles are utilised as they had been throughout the nineteenth century. Comfortable seating pieces display buttons, tufts and trims, while draperies hang at the windows. Tapestries line walls above the dado and patterned rugs cover the floor. Lambrequins adorn mantels, and cloths extend from table top to floor. As a result, the features of the room and frames of seat furniture are obscured rather than exposed. Textiles used in so generous a manner are particularly evident in Arts and Crafts interiors in England, Scandinavia and the United States. They are especially prominent in interiors furnished by enterprises having a vested interest in their use, such as Morris & Co, Liberty & Co and Associated Artists.

What distinguishes these draped and upholstered interiors as products of the Arts

Above: A Craftsman living room, illustrated in The Craftsman.

Right: An interior of the Kaufmann House by Frank Lloyd Wright, 1936.

Opposite page, bottom: An interior of Frank Lloyd Wright's house, Taliesin, built in 1911.

and Crafts Movement are the woven or printed patterns that they contain. The patterns are modelled subtly and appear relatively flat to emphasise the flatness of the planes which they cover. They tend to be stylised and carefully composed, in contrast to the undulating, naturalistic patterns of the Victorian age. Such stylisation discourages the impression conveyed by large-scale, realistic patterns – that the user is sitting or walking upon living specimens of flowers or foliage.

ALTERNATIVES TO TEXTILES

In contrast to such interiors, with their softened edges and curvilinear forms, are those that eliminate textiles wherever possible. In these relatively ascetic spaces, leather panels replace fixed upholstery, and trimmings of any sort are kept to a minimum.

Stained-glass windows substitute for draperies to screen unwanted views or to filter natural daylight, and area rugs are placed selectively (if at all) on otherwise bare floors. These interiors reveal unabashedly every angle, plane and edge. In character, they contradict the more modest, 'feminine' aesthetic characteristic of the Victorian era.

These stark, 'reformed' interiors, designed by the Greene brothers, Wright, Stickley, Gimson, Hoffmann and others, present a strict interpretation of usefulness and beauty that thrives upon eliminating every superfluous detail. By restricting the excessive use of textiles, they have established a precedent that has continued to be influential today. They are regarded by posterity as functional and proto-modern, in contrast to

Below right: Dining room, general interior, Gamble House, Pasadena, California, by Charles Sumner Greene and Henry Mather Green, 1908. Interiors by the Greene brothers contain influences ranging from vernacular to oriental. Each element is crafted allowing the exposed joinery to assume a decorative role.

other Arts and Crafts interiors that utilise fabric in a more generous fashion.

THE INFLUENCE OF OTHER STYLES

During the life span of the Arts and Crafts Movement, this varied approach to the use of colour and textiles reflected the influence of other styles and movements then in vogue. Some had little impact on Arts and Crafts interiors, while others affected everything from colour and texture to form and motif to broader issues of planning and arrangement. Among these were the Gothic Revival and High Victorian Gothic styles, the Old English, Queen Anne, Colonial and Georgian revivals,

as well as national Romanticism and the English Domestic Revival Movement.

Such influences caused some design reformers to take an eclectic approach, assembling interiors that incorporated vestiges of several contemporaneous styles. But other designers regarded such stylistic eclecticism as antithetical to the goals of the Arts and Crafts Movement. They elected to pursue a purer approach which included only the slightest trace of any outside influence.

The presence of these influences demonstrates that Arts and Crafts interiors were not created in isolation. All were products of the nineteenth century, and, as such, could not

Left: The entry/stair hall, Gamble House, Pasadena, California, by Charles Sumner Greene and Henry Mather Greene, 1908. Sculptural in finish and presence, the staircase is exquisitely crafted. The continuous moulding that defines the treads and risers resembles the trim on a Japanese hako-kaidan, *or stairway chest.*

escape the dual stronghold of revivalism and eclecticism that had dictated the evolution of style during the late eighteenth and nineteenth centuries. Nor could they resist the beckoning of more progressive trends, such as the Art Nouveau style, the *Jugendstil* or that of the Secessionist Movement. These diverse influences infused the interiors of the design-reform movements to different degrees, depending on the stylistic proclivities of architect, designer and client.

STYLISTIC ECLECTICISM

Such stylistic eclecticism is illustrated by Arts and Crafts interiors that combine medieval architectural features with Jacobean wainscoting, oriel windows and elegant furniture reminiscent of Hepplewhite and Sheraton. In others, the forthright forms of joiner and turner co-exist with pseudo-oriental finishes and sinuous Art Nouveau ornamentation. Still others explore the 'greenery-yallery' colour schemes, cluttered arrangements and oriental *bric-à-brac* promoted by the Aesthetic Movement. And in the north-eastern United States, some 'reformed' interiors blithely mix Morris chintzes and Colonial antiques with Mission-style furnishings, Japanese fans and peacock feathers. Even the idiosyncratic interiors of Mackintosh or the Greene brothers include Chinese porcelains or oriental rugs. As in all interiors, these seemingly disparate elements provide a striking contrast of age and culture which serves to enrich the whole.

The Arts and Crafts Movement strove to improve life by simplifying the home and work environment, but it presented more options than restrictions to those wishing to achieve that goal. Design reformers consequently interpreted its principles broadly and, as a result, the interiors of the design-reform movement are often more challenging to analyse than their more conservative contemporaries.

CONFLICTING INTENTIONS

The complex character of the Arts and Crafts interior can perhaps be attributed to the fact that it expresses conflicting intentions: it reflects a nostalgia for attributes from the past, while it values a fresh perspective and an original approach. It seeks to provide an environment that is both warm and comfortable, but it argues convincingly that each interior must be efficient and easy to maintain. It incorporates whimsy and subtle humour, expressing a *joie de vivre* and an appreciation of the simple things in life, but it never forgets its mission nor its sobriety of purpose. It provides a congenial background for handiwork and other personal touches, but maintains that a spare, uncluttered atmosphere alone provides quiet and repose. Such dualities reflect its pivotal position in the history of design. It embraces the time-honoured achievements of the past yet it anticipates the accomplishments of the Modern Movement.

Right: A modern reconstruction of an American Shaker interior.

ARTS AND CRAFTS
FURNITURE

An ideal of furniture made for beauty's sake as much as for use united Arts and Crafts achievement in this complex area. Architects, designers and craftsmen throughout Europe, as well as the United States, were preoccupied with the production of furniture that would play both a symbolic and a practical role in the domestic environment.

The resulting plurality of style and intention, characteristic of the whole range of Arts and Crafts production, defies simple definition. Furniture was made not only in response to changing values but also to specific needs, so that the work of Scandinavian designers, for example, is very different from that of their Viennese counterparts. Social concern could be described as one common factor, but there was no common consensus to show how that concern might be demonstrated in the design of tables and chairs, sideboards and settles. An ideal of the past and the significance of tradition also played an important role, but again we should ask ourselves: 'Whose past and what traditions were relevant to designers at the turn of the century?'

RED HOUSE

When William Morris invited his friend and colleague Philip Webb to design his first home, Red House, in 1859, the issues were more clear cut. Morris' youthful idealism had been determined by Romanticism in art and literature and by the Gothic revivalists' rejection of the machine age. The furniture that Webb and his colleagues designed for Red House represented an early attempt to create 'the blossoms of

Previous page: A chair produced by Morris & Co in ebonised wood and tapestry.

Above: A mahogany cabinet by E W Godwin and J A M Whistler, c. 1878.

Right: A wall cabinet designed by Philip Webb, c. 1861–62, and painted with scenes from the life of St George by William Morris.

the art'. Webb produced solid tables in oak, and additional furniture was designed on commission by others in those early years. The medieval inspiration was lauded when the Morris exhibit was awarded two gold medals at the International Exhibition of 1862. The jury reported: 'The general forms of the furniture . . . and the character of the details are satisfying to the archaeologist from the exactness of the imitation, at the same time that the general effect is excellent'.

WARINGTON TAYLOR

It is interesting that the first person who seems to have felt some concern about the cost and elitism of such commissions was not William Morris but Warington Taylor, the business manager of Morris & Co ('the Firm'). In 1865 Taylor told Webb: 'It is hellish wickedness to spend more than 15/- on a chair when the poor are starving in the streets'. What was needed, he wrote, was 'moveable furniture . . . something you can pull about with one hand. You can't stand fixtures now that there are no more castles'.

It is claimed that Taylor introduced the now familiar rush-seated 'Sussex chair' to the Firm, variants of which remained in production for many years. He also introduced the 'Morris easy chair' with an adjustable back. It is significant that he had found examples of these in the workshop of a Sussex carpenter, for

Above: Morris' bed at Kelmscott Manor, with hangings and cover designed by May Morris in about 1893.

Left: The 'Sussex chair', a rush-seated armchair of ebonised beechwood adapted by Webb from a traditional model.

Right: A 'Morris' adjustable-back oak armchair, adapted by Webb from a 'Sussex' type in about 1866.

Below: A 'Sussex chair' designed by Morris & Co in 1866.

Bottom right: An oak centre table made by Morris & Co. This design is attributed to Philip Webb and George Jack. It was designed in the 1880s or early 1890s.

variants of vernacular or folk furniture were to form a major part of Arts and Craft production, especially in Scandinavia, where the peasant dwelling rather than the medieval palace was to be the primary source of inspiration. Taylor was not totally scathing about his employers' efforts, however, for he approved of the fact that their furniture had no style: 'It is original, it has its own style: it is in fact Victorian'.

MORRIS & CO'S FURNITURE

As Morris became more preoccupied with wallpaper and textile design, he tended to delegate furniture commissions to his colleagues, and, in the 1880s, when George Jack, Mervyn Macartney and W A S Benson were involved in this area of the Firm's production, the furniture became more Georgian than Victorian, in keeping with the taste of their patrons, most of whom were drawn from the growing ranks of the upper-middle classes. Ford Madox Brown, however, the Pre-Raphaelite painter who was one of the Firm's founder members, produced a range of 'working men's' bedroom furniture, designed so that it could be easily copied by local carpenters and artisans.

THE CENTURY GUILD

Following the Morris precedent, several architect/designers set up their own enterprises in the 1860s and 1870s. The architect Arthur Heygate Mackmurdo, for example, established his Century Guild in 1882, designing furniture, as well as fabrics which were made for him by specialised firms. His furniture was eccentrically stylised, its essentially conventional forms frequently embellished with a fretwork motif of undulating lines. His dining chair is his most familiar design, perhaps because it has been so frequently categorised and

illustrated as proto-Art Nouveau (a claim which Mackmurdo would have rejected).

GIMSON AND BARNSLEY

The Century Guild was disbanded in 1888, but an equally short-lived group was to lead the establishment of a workshop which had

Left: An oak cabinet designed by J P Seddon and decorated with scenes from the honeymoon of King René of Anjou by Madox Brown, Burne-Jones, Morris and Rossetti, 1862.

Below: An oak writing desk by A H Mackmurdo, c. 1886.

a far more lasting influence on ideals for Arts and Crafts furniture. Kenton & Co was founded in 1890 when several young architects, including W R Lethaby, Ernest Gimson, Mervyn Macartney, Sidney Barnsley and Reginald Blomfield, set out, in the words of Blomfield, 'to produce the best possible

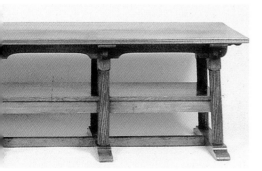

furniture of its time, with the best materials and the best workmanship'. Although this enterprise was forced to close through lack of capital in 1892, Gimson and Barnsley went on to set up on their own in rural Gloucestershire, thus establishing a dynasty of designer/craftsmen in furniture and proving against all odds that the English craft ideal could be reconciled with financial survival.

Gimson's furniture, in fact, epitomises the craft ideal of 'honest workmanship'. He is perhaps best known for his rush-seated chairs, so similar to Shaker designs, which draw directly on a vernacular tradition. But he also produced exquisite cabinets inlaid with mother-of-pearl, silver and ivory, made from native woods such as oak, elm, yew and walnut. This work, of course, replaced the earlier painted furniture of Webb and Morris

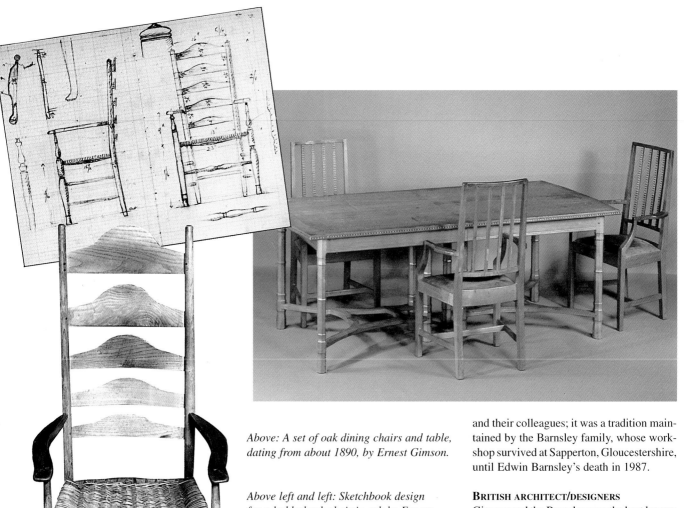

Above: A set of oak dining chairs and table, dating from about 1890, by Ernest Gimson.

Above left and left: Sketchbook design for a ladderback chair in ash by Ernest Gimson, c. 1895.

and their colleagues; it was a tradition maintained by the Barnsley family, whose workshop survived at Sapperton, Gloucestershire, until Edwin Barnsley's death in 1987.

BRITISH ARCHITECT/DESIGNERS

Gimson and the Barnsleys are the best known of the British designer/craftsmen who specialised in furniture production. Most Arts and Crafts furniture was designed by architects, either to supplement their incomes or to complement the houses they created. C F A Voysey, for example, conceived his houses as 'total design', aiming to supervise the design, or design himself, every item of their furnishing. His furniture, like his architecture, is deceptively simple and understated – 'poor people's furniture for the rich', according to the claims of the more cynical. Edwin Lutyens and, above all, Baillie Scott designed or conceived furniture and interiors for 'dream houses' which were internationally admired and emulated, representing an ideal of domesticity that struck a chord among the middle classes throughout Europe and the United States.

SCANDINAVIAN ARTS AND CRAFTS FURNITURE

The home was also the focus for an ideal of design and craftsmanship in Sweden at the turn of the century. Ellen Key, the Swedish sociologist and aesthetician, expounded the principle in her book *Beauty for All* in 1897: 'Things must . . . fulfil their purpose in a simple and expressive manner, and without this they do not achieve beauty even if they satisfy practical requirements'.

Sweden was the most industrialised of the Scandinavian countries in the nineteenth century and had promoted schemes for design reform since the 1840s. These reform schemes were co-ordinated by the Swedish Society for Craft and Design (Svenska Slojdforeningen), which was launched in 1845. With its motto 'Swedish handicraft is the father of Swedish independence', Svensk Form (as it is now known) concentrated on essentially practical programmes which encouraged self-sufficiency in local industries and enterprises.

By the 1890s, when the 'renaissance' associated with Art Nouveau, as well as with the Arts and Crafts Movement, was spreading throughout Europe, Sweden already had an established tradition of design reform on which to draw. It also had a surviving tradition of local or vernacular craftsmanship, especially in the textile and furniture industries, a tradition which was studied and preserved in museums and art schools. As far as the country's furniture production was concerned, local light industries, such as those in the

Left: A round oak table by Heal & Sons, London. Heals retailed furniture to the middle classes.

Below: 'Brita's Forty Winks', illustration for Ett Hem *by Carl Larsson, 1899.*

province of Smaland, were able to maintain their output of low-cost and unpretentious designs for the domestic market.

CARL LARSSON

One house in particular provided a focus for Swedish domestic ideals in the 1890s: the country home of the painter Carl Larsson, Sundborn. One summer, Larsson painted his house and family; these watercolours were exhibited in the Industrial Exhibition in Stockholm in 1897 and aroused so much interest that they were published in a book two years later. *Ett Hem* [*A Home*] set the style for a generation. Larsson's 'best' furniture dated from the eighteenth century, whereas the workaday furniture could have been produced on his own estate. It was these simpler objects which attracted the interest of Swedish furniture designers. Carl Westmann, for example, designed furniture in the spirit of *Ett Hem* and, like Eric Josephson, produced designs for 'workers' furniture'.

CARL WESTMANN AND ALF WALLENDER

Westmann was one of the most prolific furniture designers during this period and, besides drawing on vernacular traditions, was also obviously influenced by the work of the British, Belgians and Viennese. Alf Wallender, who is probably best known for his work in ceramics for Rorstrand, also designed simple furniture which was exhibited in workers' institutes, as well as more elaborate pieces for private commissions.

CARL MALMSTEN

Carl Malmsten, the winner of several prizes in a competition for furniture for Stockholm's town hall, set up his own workshop and embarked on a prestigious and controversial career as a furniture designer. He produced experimental pieces as well as luxurious, inlaid cabinets, but also concentrated on simple designs in the craft tradition, work which was celebrated in the 1950s when 'Swedish Grace' enjoyed international prestige.

FINNISH FURNITURE

Within the context of Scandinavian developments, the Finnish interpretation of Arts and Crafts ideals was unique. Finland had been part of the Swedish Empire until the beginning of the nineteenth century, when it came under the jurisdiction of Russia. Towards the end of the nineteenth century, however,

the Finns began to discover their identity. The Friends of Finnish Handicraft was established in 1879 and the country's architects and designers also looked to folk architecture.

At the Paris World Fair of 1900, the Finnish Pavilion, which included work by Louis Sparre (who was, in fact, Swedish), was awarded several medals. Before working on the World Fair pavilion, Sparre had produced designs for 'Finnish-style dining-room furniture' and in 1897 had set up the Iris Workshops in Porvoo for the production of textiles, ceramics and furniture. Sparre designed the 'Iris' furniture which was marketed in Finland and St Petersburg, Russia.

Opposite: An interior by Louis Sparre, Finland, c. 1903.

Below left: A white-painted table by Charles Rennie Mackintosh, Scotland. Elegant and innovatory designs such as these were highly acclaimed on the European continent; they were considered 'decadent', however, by the traditionalists of the English Arts and Crafts Movement.

Above: A table and chair with stencilled canvas back by Charles Rennie Mackintosh, c. 1901.

Right: An armchair veneered in amboyna wood, designed by Koloman Moser, 1904.

HVITTRASK

One of the most celebrated special architectural commissions in Finland was Hvittrask, buildings by Saarinen, Gesellius and Lindgren, used as studios and homes for their families. Hvittrask was furnished throughout with designs by the trio and Sparre. Saarinen designed all the furniture for the main building; the chairs in the living room and dining area are based on traditional prototypes, while the bedroom furniture was obviously inspired by the work of the Scottish designer Charles Rennie Mackintosh.

VIENNA SECESSION FURNITURE

Mackintosh's work caused a sensation in Vienna when it was exhibited at the Vienna Secession Exhibition of 1900. The impetus for the formation of the Wiener Werkstätte in 1903 was certainly based on the English precedent and Josef Hoffmann's 'manifesto' for the workshops has a distinctly Arts and Crafts ring: 'Our point of departure is purpose: utility is our prime consideration'. How far Vienna Secession furniture and design can be defined as Arts and Crafts is debatable, however.

Koloman Moser, for example, designed

some of the most luxurious pieces associated with the group. His magnificent cabinets, with their elaborate veneers and inlays, belong to the grand traditions of cabinet-making. His more starkly geometrical designs, however, many of them in black and white, are innovative and iconoclastic.

Adolf Loos, the architect, designer and polemicist, loathed the elitism that came to be associated with Vienna Secession work. The furniture he designed was unpretentious and functional, demonstrating his understanding of the nature of materials and the relationship of material to form. These qualities can be related to the machine, as well as to craft production, and it is significant that Loos used Thonet bentwood chairs in several of his commissions. One of the first was for

the Café Museum in Vienna in 1899: the tables have solid bentwood bases and marble tops; his billiard table has brass fittings, a device he frequently employed to protect chair legs; and the chairs are standard designs by Thonet.

THONET BENTWOOD CHAIRS

Thonet bentwood chairs had been in production since the 1840s, when Michael Thonet took out his first patents for bending and reshaping strips of wood. In the 1850s the firm began to expand and by the end of the century Thonet had become a household name: its familiar chairs were not only used in cafés throughout Europe but were also exported to the United States. The Vienna Secession designers had work produced by Thonet, and when Le Courbusier was equipping his

Above: A nineteenth-century Shaker chair. Shaker furniture anticipated many of the concerns of the Arts and Crafts Movement in the United States.

Left: 'A Craftsman Dining Room', as featured in The Craftsman, *USA, Gustav Stickley, c. 1904. 'Craftsman' interiors were designed to combine easily massproduced fittings with a homely and comfortable atmosphere.*

Above and right: Gustav Stickley is best known for his strong, sturdy designs. These fall-front desks are typical, made of an indigenous wood, oak, in a plain and simple 'non-style'.

Pavilion de L'Esprit Nouveau for the Paris Exhibition of 1925 he included Thonet dining chairs. Thonet relied on machine processes to produce furniture which achieved the egalitarian ideals of the craft tradition: it was simple, functional and unpretentious. Above all, the standard ranges were inexpensive and therefore available to all.

GERMAN FURNITURE

The need for inexpensive, machine-produced furniture which was expressive of craft values was also acknowledged in Germany. In 1907 an organisation called the Deutsche Werkbund was established in Munich, aimed at 'the improvement of industrial products through the collaboration of art, industry and craft'. The organisation included manufacturers among its members, and associated organisations, such as the Dresden and Munich Werkstätte, began to revise their attitudes towards machine production. In Dresden, the Vereinigte Werkstätte für Kunst in Handwerk was founded in 1898 by Karl Schmidt, who had been trained as a carpenter.

TYPENMÖBEL

Among the designers working for Schmidt's successful furniture workshop at Hellerau was Richard Riemerschmid, whose early furniture included cabinets and bureaux with elaborate veneers and inlays. In 1907, however, the workshops began to concentrate on serial or semi-mass production and introduced ranges of *Typenmöbel* ('type furniture') – chairs and cabinets made from standardised components. The financial success of these enabled the workshops to amalgamate with the Munich Werkstätte and together they built a 'garden city' at Hellerau, where the furniture workshops remained the focus of the community.

Bruno Paul, a founder member of the Munich Werkstätte, was involved in the design and production of *Typenmöbel*. He conceived his first furniture for his own house, which led to commissions from private clients. In 1908 he began to design furniture which could be produced by semi-mass-production techniques, concentrating on a limited number of designs. The components of his chairs, tables and cabinets were standardised, but were produced in different woods and finishes so that a unity of design could be demonstrated throughout a house.

These experiments in standardisation succeeded in breaking the barrier of elitism. Although only the middle classes could afford it in Germany, several large-scale industries, such as Krupps and AEG, furnished their workers' houses with designs based on similar principles.

ARTS AND CRAFTS FURNITURE IN AMERICA

The impact of British Arts and Crafts ideals for furniture on American designers is best epitomised by the works and philosophy of Gustav Stickley, editor of the magazine *The Craftsman* (1901–16). When he set up his own workshops with his brothers at Binghamton, New York, it was Shaker simplicity that he tried to emulate, however. It was not until 1899, when, now a convert to the ideals of Ruskin and Morris, he formed the Gustav Stickley Company in Eastwood, New York, that he consolidated his own ideas. Stickley is best known for his 'Mission' furniture: strong, sturdy designs, mainly in oak, which were intended to evoke the 'simple life' of the early pioneers. The success of this furniture and its adaptability to machine production meant that he had many competitors. In 1900 he launched United Crafts in the Craftsman Building in Syracuse, organised along co-operative lines.

Above: A sideboard produced by the workshops of Gustav Stickley, of oak and oak veneer with hammered copper hinges and handles, c. 1910–16.

Left: A photograph published in The Craftsman *of Gustav Stickley's Craftsman Workshops, c. 1902–3.*

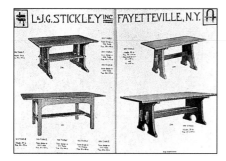

Above: Pages from the L & J G Stickley catalogue, 1922. L and J G Stickley, brothers of Gustav Stickley, set up a rival enterprise in 1900.

Right: A waste-paper basket designed by Charles Rohlfs made of American white oak with an attached leather bag, c. 1910.

Commercial success, however, encouraged him to overextend his empire and he eventually became bankrupt.

ELBERT HUBBARD AND CHARLES ROHLFS

Also designing furniture during this period was Elbert Hubbard, who established his Roycroft Guild venture in East Aurora, New York. In 1897 he introduced a line of furniture very similar to Stickley's 'Mission' range, but his enthusiasm was condemned as naïvely populist. The furniture made by another Buffalo craftsman at the turn of the century was more in keeping with the

mainstream Arts and Crafts tradition. Charles Rohlfs' early pieces were also in the 'Mission' style. Most of his work, however, was elaborately carved and pierced, and he was one of the few American furniture-makers to use Art Nouveau ornamentation.

THE GREENE BROTHERS

American architects, too, made a significant contribution to Arts and Crafts furniture design. The Greene brothers' Gamble House, in Pasadena, California, built between 1908 and 1909, is an example of 'total design'. Charles Sumner Greene, like so many of his contemporaries, had made the pilgrimage to England, and the furniture that he and his brother Henry Mather Greene produced is a celebration of an ideal of the home. Like Mackintosh's, the

Left: The morning room at Standen; the table in the foreground is by Philip Webb.

Below: A cabinet and chair by the Greene brothers for the Charles M Pratt house, Ojai Valley, California, c. 1909. The furniture was made by Peter Hall, a cabinetmaker who worked with the brothers.

Right: An armchair designed by Frank Lloyd Wright.

Below: A side chair by Frank Lloyd Wright for the Aline Barnsdell house, Los Angeles, 1920.

work of the Greene brothers displayed obvious Chinese influences, including the curved splats borrowed for the Chippendale style. But Japan, they felt, had transformed carpentry into art, and their work is distinguished by this ideal.

FRANK LLOYD WRIGHT

Frank Lloyd Wright also designed furniture within an architectural context. When he conceived the Robie house and its furniture in 1908, the early associations of his work with the 'Missions' and the early pioneers were abandoned. Wright's furniture was designed to make a statement about the relationship of form to space. It is therefore no coincidence that the Dutch designer Gerrit Rietveld was asked shortly before World War I to reproduce some of Wright's furniture for an avant-garde house in The Netherlands. Wright transformed the Arts and Crafts aesthetic to complement that 'geometric sense of things' that is so characteristic of Modern Movement achievements.

ARTS AND CRAFTS
METALWORK

Previous page: A Liberty & Co 'Cymric' silver and enamel covered box, 1900.

Below right: Silver cutlery by Josef Hoffmann for the Wiener Werkstätte, Austria, 1903–4. This pleasantly functional cutlery is closely related to that designed by Charles Rennie Mackintosh in 1901 for the Ingram Street Tea Rooms, Glasgow, Scotland.

The character of most materials is greatly determined by its limitations. Metals can be made to do almost anything, from shaping a jug to roofing a steeple, and their nature is a matter of interpretation. The Arts and Crafts Movement formed its own arbitrary rules and taboos about metals and the way in which they should be handled – rules that its adherents frequently ignored to good effect.

Gold, silver and bronze might be cast, but iron never. Wrought iron should not be bolted or welded. Saw-piercing was *infra dig*, platinum frowned upon; gems, companions to the noble metals, should be semi-precious and uncut. No machinery should be used, a prohibition which, in a modern world, it was impossible to observe to the letter. On the other hand, Arts and Crafts designers played havoc with orthodox trade practices by mixing base and precious metals, setting domestic silverware with gems and enamels and embellishing furniture with decorative metal plaques and the sort of hinges used on outhouses.

HANDCRAFT VERSUS MACHINE PRODUCTION
Metal has no visible grain, unlike wood or leather, and mechanical methods cannot reveal its hidden nature. Arts and Crafts designers set great store by the hammer finish, the skin of callused metal that grows under the worker's hand in the rough-and-tumble

Left: A 'Tudric' tea set designed for Liberty & Co by Archibald Knox, 1904.

Below: A Morris & Co whistling kettle made of copper and brass. It is an example of simplicity of design which anticipates the work of the Deutscher Werkbund and the Bauhaus in Germany.

of creation. The artist/craftsman tolerated inequalities of surface or form – even encouraged them: they held the eye in a way that the precision and symmetry of a machined object could never do.

The versatility of the metals suited them to multiple production, and in the first half of the nineteenth century mechanical techniques largely took over from handcraft. Wrought iron was almost entirely replaced by cast iron in architecture and the home. Hollow-ware, instead of being hand-beaten into shape over an iron stake, was either 'spun' – squeezed into shape on a lathe against a suitably formed 'chuck' – or stamped out on a press. Jewellery, too, was punched out wholesale. Competition was savage and production meant that the vital connections between designer and workman and workman and metal were being loosened; it was these bonds that Arts and Crafts longed to see remade.

IRONWORK

By the middle of the nineteenth century, the craft of wrought ironwork was fast giving way to cast iron in the decorative arts. As a decorative medium, cast iron had serious limitations. Its intense heat in the molten state often caused it to burn the surface of the sand mould when it was poured, with a consequent loss of depth and precision. Nor was there any chance of chasing in the lost detail with a hammer and chisel, cast iron being too brittle. The traditional way in which to create relief in ironwork was by building it up layer by layer in laminations of pierced and fretted metal, or by forging, filing and chiselling it into shape, methods which gave great richness of detail but were quite unsuited to multiple production. The most effective use of cast iron in the decorative arts is in the simple, rhythmic patterns seen in railings and balustrades.

WROUGHT IRON

A wave of church restoration in the second part of the nineteenth century encouraged the revival of wrought ironwork. Architects such as Sir George Gilbert Scott replaced the vanished screens of medieval church buildings with versions of their own. The fashion for wrought iron grew as the Arts and Crafts

Right: A silver-gilt and enamel candlestick by A W N Pugin, England.

Below: A candlestick of forged iron by Ernest Gimson and Alfred Bucknell, England, c. 1908. A combination of sound engineering and good design utilises the characteristics of the metal simply and naturally.

Movement gained momentum, particularly in fire irons for the fashionable inglenook, to which the heat-resistant metal was well suited. The furniture-maker Ernest Gimson designed fire irons to be made up in brass and iron by Alfred Bucknell, a son of the village blacksmith of Tunley, Gloucestershire. Bucknell could breathe life into iron by the simplest possible means, using no more decoration than a few licks with the file or punch. He had an intuitive understanding of the plastic qualities of forged iron and his partnership with Gimson was close.

CHARLES RENNIE MACKINTOSH

Although iron is liable to corrosion and needs to be painted to protect it from the weather, its great strength makes it suitable for architectural work. Cryptic and elegant, Charles Rennie Mackintosh's ironwork for the Glasgow School of Art remains the subject of discussion. The brackets to the studio windows in the north-western façade combine support and decoration with the prosaic function of holding up the window-cleaner's planks. Their tops end in curious knot motifs which have been compared with the hilt of a Scottish broadsword. The railings below are tipped with the spear-shaped leaves which C F A Voysey introduced and are supported by tall iron staffs crested with pierced roundels which have been identified as *mon,* Japanese heraldic shields.

Inside the building, a balustrade is strengthened by vertical bands of iron punched with oval holes, like those in a well-worn harness. The T-girders supporting the roof are split and scrolled into knots, a device in the true Arts and Crafts spirit which emphasises rather than disguises the nature of the object. The ironwork gives the school an embattled look, as though it were defending the Glasgow arts against all-comers.

ANTONIO GAUDÍ

Antonio Gaudí, architect of the fantastic cathedral of the Sagrada Familia in Barcelona, understood how light could be interrupted and transformed by a skeletal membrane of wrought iron. The iron gates which he made for the grotto in the Parc Güell, with their meandering patterns and paired wing forms, were intended to be seen looking out against the harsh Catalan light. Gaudí was the son of a coppersmith of the city of Reus in Tarragona and had grown up with metalwork and metal-workers, and this total familiarity with the medium allowed him to push the metal to its limits. His iron drifts, twirls, squirms and tangles; it beguiles and repels, soothes and lacerates, but it always behaves like iron. The wings of the Jabberwock-like guardian of his dragon gate were made of iron mesh to give them a vibrant translucency. The gates of the entrance to the Mila House in Barcelona were designed like the veining of a leaf or an insect's wing and glazed.

SAM YELLIN

In the United States, the best ironwork was made in commercial workshops. There was a keen demand for hand-wrought architectural ironwork in America during the first third of the twentieth century and superb work was done by such craftsmen as Frank Koralewsky in Boston, Cyril Colnik in Milwaukee and the Polish-born Samuel Yellin in Philadelphia. A sensitive and cultivated designer, much of Yellin's work was based on medieval origi-nals, using the same traditional techniques – the collared joints not only clenching the scroll-work together but also picking out its melodic pattern with a simple counterpoint. Although he used the latest technology, Yelling believed that 'there is only one way to make good deco-rative ironwork and that is with the hammer at the anvil . . .'

FRANK KORALEWSKY

Frank Koralewsky was an immigrant who had served his apprenticeship in the Pomeranian town of Stralsund. It was his belief that it was possible to match the magnificent metalwork of the late Middle Ages and Renaissance. To prove his point, he devoted his spare time for six or seven years to producing his handsome

and intricate *'Schneewittchen'* lock, which retold the fairy tale of Snow White. Relief panels inlaid with gold, silver and bronze illus-trated episodes in the story and even the hidden parts of the lock were decorated.

LOUIS SULLIVAN

Although the use of cast iron ran squarely against the doctrines of the Arts and Crafts Movement, in the hands of the Chicago archi-tect Louis Sullivan the medium transcended its own nature. The buildings he designed were often richly and fantastically decorated in a distinctive style which combined Renaissance and Gothic elements with angularities and

Left: Detail, ironwork from the north front of the Glasgow School of Art by Charles Rennie Mackintosh, 1897 to 1899. The tall staff rising above the railings is decorated with a pierced disc.

Below: Detail, dragon gate, by Antonio Gaudí for the Güell Estate, Barcelona, 1884. The wrought-ironwork was carried out in the workshops of a Barcelona locksmith under Gaudí's supervision.

Above: Detail, Carson Pirie Scott store, Chicago, by Louis Sullivan, 1899–1904. Using plaster models and refined moulding techniques, the American ironfounders at the turn of the century achieved the excellence of detail and surface usually associated with cire-perdue *bronze casting.*

Right: An electric kettle for AEG designed by Peter Behrens in Germany, c. *1908.*

webbed plane surfaces. The magnificent Carson Pirie Scott department store in Chicago was ornamented in this way. The intention was to set the display windows almost like jewels in frames of delicate, cast-iron ornamentation. No more than (½" (1cm) thick, the decoration combined meticulous detail with deep modelling, some of it even freestanding.

COPPER

The warm glow of copper was a part of the ambience of the Arts and Crafts home. Copper is easy to work and so appeals strongly to the amateur. John Pearson, of the Guild and School of Handicrafts, was claimed by Ashbee to have been an unemployed potter from the De Morgan factory who had taught himself copperwork by studying it in the British Museum. His large copper platters were boldly ornamented with fishes and birds and such guild motifs as the ship and peacock.

Birmingham was a great centre for the mass-production of brass and copper goods, turning out everything from bedsteads to cooking pots. The Birmingham Guild of Handicrafts was founded in 1890 on the principles laid down by Ashbee and Morris. No machinery was used except the lathe, essential for the production of domestic light fittings in which the guild specialised. Lugs, handles and other additions fitted to its vessels were often fixed with rivets; silver boxes were assembled in the same way.

Domestic copperwork was even more popular in the United States than in Britain, although there were many points of comparison in the work produced on both sides of the Atlantic. The pieces produced by the Roycroft Guild's copper workshop, for example, demonstrate their links with the British Arts and Crafts Movement in their robust, hammer-finished copperwork with

exposed rivet heads. Dirk Van Erp began his career as an art metalworker by hammering brass shell cases into vases. These found a ready market and in 1908 he opened a shop in Oakland before beginning a short-lived partnership with Eleanor D'Arcy Gaw, a designer, weaver and metalworker who had trained with Ashbee, creating a highly successful range of ornamental copperware, including the table lamps with tinted isinglass shades for which Van Erp is best known.

COPPER LAMPS

The introduction of electricity to the home offered opportunities and challenges to the designer. In 1895 electricity was installed in Ashbee's home, the Magpie and Stump, in Chelsea. The lamps hung by strands of twisted wires from roses of beaten metal or were grouped with pendent spheres of glowing, translucent enamel. For the Glasgow School

of Art, Mackintosh made a fall of 13 copper lamps, each like a tower pierced with a grid of square windows and lined with purple glass. In the lecture theatre, his boat-shaped lampshades of hammered brass exuded just enough light for note-taking.

BRASS

Brass is less easily raised into hollow-ware than copper and its traditional use has always been in illumination. Some of Bucknell and Gimson's finest work is to be seen in their brass candle sconces, the flat backplates pierced with simple, vigorous decoration.

Robert Riddle Jarvie of Chicago specialised in candlesticks and lanterns. His popular candlesticks, sold in his Jarvie Shop, were typically modelled in forms which subtly suggest tall-stemmed flowers, cast in brass, copper or bronze and either brush-finished or patinated. He later made silver presentation pieces.

True to the Arts and Crafts dictum that the function of an object should be celebrated rather than hidden, a great deal of care was given to hinges and fittings around the home. Copper was rather soft for this purpose, but hinges were often made in brass. The hinges that Voysey designed for William Morris'

Above: A copper repoussé *vase from the workshops of the Keswick School of Industrial Art, England,* c. *1900. The simple,* repoussé *decoration is typical of the work of the school.*

Left: A copper urn by Frank Lloyd Wright, made by James A Miller, Chicago, c. *1900. The formal decoration of* repoussé *panelling was designed as a complement to Wright's geometrical interiors.*

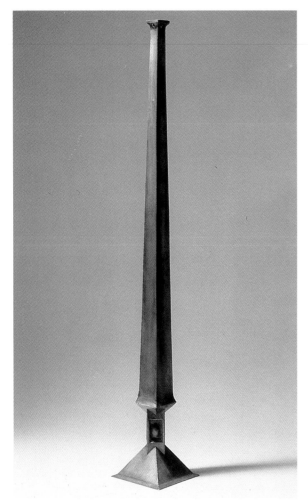

Above: A copper 'weed vase' designed by Frank Lloyd Wright, made by James A Miller, Chicago, c. 1894.

Above right: A copper electric desk lamp by Dirk Van Erp, USA, c. 1901.

'Kelmscott Chaucer Cabinet', with their heart-shaped tips and openwork decoration of birds, are a fine example of his work. Mackintosh designed shallow *repoussé* metal plaques to decorate his furniture and interiors, using the same vocabulary as in his other two-dimensional designs: ellipses, peacock eyes

and the familiar girls.

Mackintosh's influence is seen strongly in the early metalwork designed by Josef Hoffmann for the Wiener Werkstätte, particularly the window-like piercing, the strong perpendiculars and 90° angles. Although Glasgow designs remained significant in the

Wiener Werkstätte, after Koloman Moser left in 1906 they gave ground to an agreeably blowsy Viennese style: brass and silver tea sets, smoking sets and fruit bowls, their tapered and fluted bodies like well-boned corsets, the handles cusped like Cupid's bows.

TIFFANY & CO

At the 1878 Paris Exposition, the New York firm of Tiffany & Co showed wares made of base-metal alloys laminated with fine gold and/or silver, causing a sensation by breaking a Western convention against marrying the base and noble metals. Eccentric, eclectic and empirical, Tiffany & Co broke rules; invented new ones; built altar candlesticks of thick bronze wire and set them with uncut quartz pebbles; and made a Native American loving cup of pink metal with handles of sheep horns. The firm began experimenting with enamel before 1900 as a decoration for the bases of lamps. The enamelled copper vessels it made

Above: A metal lampshade designed by Charles Rennie Mackintosh, c. 1900.

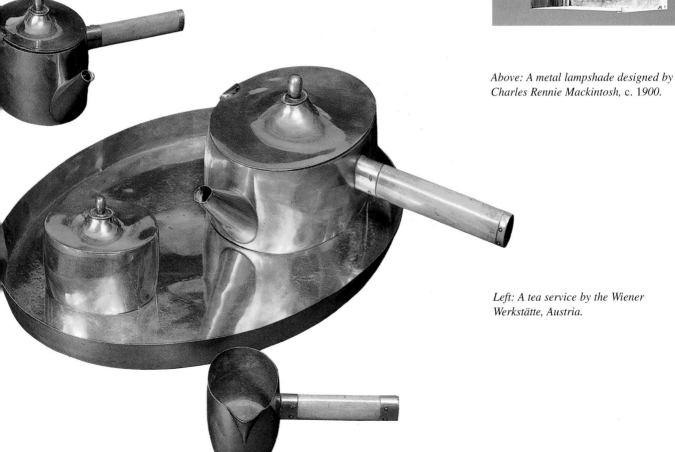

Left: A tea service by the Wiener Werkstätte, Austria.

Right: A brass tea set, with handles of pale wood, by Josef Hoffmann for the Wiener Werkstätte, c. 1905.

Below: A silver vase by Josef Hoffmann for the Wiener Werkstätte, c. 1904.

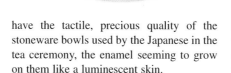

have the tactile, precious quality of the stoneware bowls used by the Japanese in the tea ceremony, the enamel seeming to grow on them like a luminescent skin.

GOLD AND SILVER
Arts and Crafts jewellers and silversmiths were skilled, versatile and sensitive and evolved a great variety of styles. Nevertheless, a 'family' likeness runs through their work. Most of their work was in silver, with some jewellery in 18-carat gold. Platinum was hardly ever used, but steel, copper and aluminium also sometimes appear in jewellery.

There was a characteristic aversion to the slick finish. The hammered surface was universal in silver and sometimes, instead of being polished, the metal was lightly rubbed with fine emery. Riveting often replaced soldering. Gems and enamels were set quite promiscuously in both jewellery and silverware, but according to strict conventions. The domed cabochon style of cutting was almost invariably used in simple, close settings, giving a natural, spontaneous effect, as though the stones were budding from the metal. The palette was restricted to the more subdued, semi-precious stones, especially opal, moonstone, veined turquoise matrix, cat's eye, garnet, amethyst and the irregularly shaped Mississippi pearl; star rubies and sapphires were acceptable. The purpose was not simply to lend colour to the object, but also a mood of mystery and glamour.

BOTANICAL DESIGNS

The Art of Decorative Design by Christopher Dresser, a trained botanist, encouraged jewellers and metalworkers to seek inspiration in living plants. The naturalistic botanical designs – unassuming jewels of lush, willowy foliage, touched with enamel and inhabited by little birds – of the British jewellers Arthur and Georgina Gaskin had many imitators. Bernard Cuzner, who headed the metalwork department of the Birmingham School of Art, also used botanical motifs.

Beautifully observed and realised, London architect Henry Wilson's stylised roses, figs and pomegranates are not so much caricatures of nature as tokens of her power. His work is not only finely conceived but elegantly engineered. The borders of chequered enamel give Wilson's jewels a heraldic feeling, while animals and finely modelled human figures

Below: A Liberty & Co silver and enamel casket by Archibald Know, 1903.

Above right: A candlestick in painted copper, brass and wood by Christopher Dresser, made by Perry & Co, 1883.

Above: A christening mug made for Lord David Cecil by members of the Guild of Handicraft, 1902.

also appear in his work.

The coolly stylised jewels that Otto Czeschka designed for the Wiener Werkstätte were pretty and wearable two-dimensional patterns of holly-like leaves and toy birds, set with random groupings of cabochon gems and composed with arrangements of thin chain.

TIFFANY & CO AND ARTHUR STONE
Wild flowers – dandelion, nightshade, blackberry – were prominent among the art jewellery

made by Tiffany & Co before World War I. The collection also included Byzantine and Art Nouveau designs, and the gems with which the pieces were set were often of American origin.

The simplicity and nearness to nature of the work of Arthur J Stone was greatly admired in Europe. His plain, classical silver is clearly in the New England tradition. Some of his work is decorated with finely observed chasings of plants; the barbed leaves of the arrowhead were particular favourites. He carried

Above: A turquoise-matrix, gold and enamel brooch by C R Ashbee, c. 1899.

Top right: Jessie M King's silver and enamel pendant, c. 1902.

Right: An enamelled brooch-pendant by Henry Wilson, c. 1913.

Above: A glass decanter with silver mounts by C R Ashbee, c. 1904–5.

Above right: A silver-mounted jug by C R Ashbee at the Guild of Handicraft, c. 1900; green glass by Powell's of Whitefriars.

out the chasing himself, occasionally adding touches of gold inlay. Even the hammer finish on his silver was barely perceptible.

EIGHTEENTH-CENTURY FASHIONS

Eighteenth-century fashions were popular with most Edwardians and they also appear to have infiltrated the silverware of the Arts and Crafts Movement. The most distinctive work by Arthur Dixon, of the Birmingham Guild of Handicraft, is in the Queen Anne style

– round-bodied vessels, vases, jugs, teapots and coffee pots with sensible fruitwood knobs and handles, devoid of any decoration other than a hammer finish.

Tiffany & Co launched a fine range of table silver which was inspired by Queen Anne design, as was the simple, panelled and globular domestic silver produced and sold in her Chicago Kalo shops by Clara Barck Welles. In Copenhagen, Denmark, Georg Jensen's rich but unpretentious domestic silver, with its plump, hand-hammered surfaces ornamented with succulent clusters of fruits and flowers, evokes the bourgeois comforts of the Age of Reason.

CLASSICAL INFLUENCES

Since the prophets of the Arts and Crafts revival were mainly gentlemen of classical education, the influence of antiquity is inescapable. The bowl that Ashbee designed for jam or butter, with its round, shallow body, double handles and trumpet-shaped foot, has features in common with Greek drinking vessels. This enchantingly simple but striking design, with its wide-looped handles which part at the top

and cling to the body with little suckers, is an Arts and Crafts classic and was successfully imitated by Marcus & Co of New York. For the most part, it was the nature worship of antiquity that appealed to Arts and Crafts designers. Vines, figs and pomegranates often appeared in jewellery, as did the god Pan.

WILLIAM BURGES

Although 'Brummagem Gothic' was a powerful force in nineteenth-century decoration, the medieval element in Arts and Crafts came in a direct line of descent from Pugin. The silver designs of his disciple, William Burges, were as eccentric as his

Below: A dessert service, silver set with enamel and gems, by William Burges for the Marquess of Bute, made by Barkentin and Krall, England, 1880–81. The style is an architectural Gothic, and the bottom of each branch is formed as a tiny, otter-like head, with a carnelian-bead pendant from its jaws.

Above: An enamelled triptych by Alexander Fisher, c. 1900.

personality. Brilliantly playful and idiosyncratic, totally unlike Pugin's chaste silver, they team with living creatures – cats, spiders, mermaids and mice. He often blended bizarre assemblages of coins, enamels, Chinese hardstone carvings and Japanese ivories and contrasted suave engraving with sharp relief and quiet *champlevé* enamel with showy *émail en ronde bosse* in a way that makes every element act as the antidote to the another.

THE JAPANESE INFLUENCE

Western designers went to visit Japan and Japanese craftsmen came to teach enamelling and metalwork, exerting a deep influence on such leading figures as Mackintosh and Dresser. Tiffany & Co began to make silver decorated in the Japanese style, hammer finished and applied with gold and copper butterflies, bottle-gourd vines, wistaria and subaqueous waterscapes full of fishes, frogs and weeds. The firm made bowls and vases of Japanese inlaid silver and copper which at the same time reproduced the baskets used by the Hopi, Zuni and Navajo tribes.

The revival of enamelling began in France, and it was Dalpeyrat of Sèvres who introduced enamel to British Arts and Crafts. In 1886 he gave a series of demonstrations to students in London, including Alexander Fisher. Fisher's painted enamels are of extraordinary quality, the colours rich and subtly graduated. In the exquisite 'Love Cup' jewel by the Edinburgh-based Phoebe Traquair, the scene is finite and complete. Her enamels have the shimmering mystery of Celtic legend.